I'M A GLOBAL CITIZEN

CARING for the ENVIRONMENT

Written by Georgia Amson-Bradshaw

Illustrated by David Broadbent

W

3013021929966 5

Franklin Watts
First published in Great Britain in 2019 by The Watts Publishing Group
Copyright © The Watts Publishing Group, 2019

 Produced for Franklin Watts by
White-Thomson Publishing Ltd
www.wtpub.co.uk

ISBN (HB): 978 1 4451 6399 4
ISBN (PB): 978 1 4451 6400 7

Series Editor: Georgia Amson-Bradshaw
Series Designer: David Broadbent
All Illustrations by: David Broadbent

Printed in Dubai

Franklin Watts
An imprint of
Hachette Children's Group
Part of The Watts Publishing Group
Carmelite House
50 Victoria Embankment
London EC4Y 0DZ

An Hachette UK Company
www.hachette.co.uk
www.franklinwatts.co.uk

Facts, figures and dates were correct when going to press.

CONTENTS

Look out for this little book symbol to find definitions of important words. Other definitions can be found in the glossary on page 30.

What is the environment?

What do you think of when you think about 'the environment'? Do you think of fields and oceans, perhaps faraway forests full of wild animals and tropical birds? These things are part of the environment, but it's much more than that!

People are animals, too

Although we don't tend to think of it this way, human beings are animals too. Like trees and birds, we are also part of nature. Even in the middle of a big city, we are surrounded by the natural world, from the air we breathe, to the soil and rocks in the ground beneath our feet.

Being part of the natural world means that we rely on nature's systems to support us. From trees and insects, to the soil itself – we depend on nature for our survival. We can't live without the environment, but we often act as though we can, by polluting the Earth and using up resources such as land and water.

Problems in the environment

There are a lot of big, man-made problems facing us and the rest of the natural world right now. Climate change (see pages 6–7) is having a lot of impact around the globe. Important plants and animals are dying off (see pages 9–10), and pollution is damaging many natural habitats (see page 14–15).

Habitat
The home of a plant or animal.

Changing our behaviour

We can take better care of the planet, allowing all living things – including ourselves – to thrive. In order to do better, we will have to change our behaviour. Some things we can do as individuals, and some things we need to do together, but fortunately a healthy environment full of happy people and animals is within our power to achieve.

What is climate change?

One of the biggest ways that human beings are currently damaging the environment is through climate change. This is the disruption of weather patterns around the world as a result of certain gases being released into the atmosphere through human activity.

The atmosphere

The Earth is surrounded by a thin layer of gases, called the atmosphere. These gases are what protect life on Earth. They contain the oxygen that we breathe, and they also keep the planet's temperature stable. They protect us from the harshest of the Sun's rays, but they also trap warmth from the Sun — like a greenhouse.

Atmosphere
The atmosphere is made up of a mixture of gases, including nitrogen, oxygen and carbon dioxide (CO_2). Carbon dioxide is the gas that is mostly responsible for trapping heat, so we call it a 'greenhouse gas'.

Too much CO$_2$

For the last few hundred years, we have been adding more and more CO$_2$ to the atmosphere by burning fossil fuels such as coal, oil and petrol. This means the atmosphere is trapping more and more of the Sun's heat.

The atmosphere protects us from the strongest rays.

Greenhouse gases trap some of the Sun's heat.

More droughts and floods

The hotter the air on Earth is, the more water vapour it can hold before it finally reaches the point where the water condenses and starts to fall as rain. As a result, some places around the world are getting less and less rain, as the hotter air never gets cold enough for rain to fall. This can cause drought. In other areas, the air is storing up extra water before finally dropping it, causing very heavy rainstorms and flooding.

Living in a changing climate

The changes to weather patterns around the world are already having a big impact on people and other living things. Air temperatures and amounts of rainfall affect where and when plants can grow, and plants form the basis of all food chains. This has a knock-on impact on other living things.

Farming

For farmers to grow the fruit, vegetables and grains that we eat, they need the right weather. They need the Sun to shine at the right time to ripen the crops, and the right amount of rain to fall so that their plants don't either dry out, or get flooded and die. Climate change is stopping farmers from being able to grow their crops, and in some places this is already leading to food shortages.

Flooding

Hotter global temperatures are causing the ice at the Earth's poles to melt. This is making sea levels rise around the world. Heavier rainfall is also leading to flooding. Coastal areas are particularly at risk. Flooding can destroy people's homes, and even force them to move to other areas.

Wildlife

Natural vegetation also struggles with changing temperatures and weather patterns, as most species can't adapt quickly enough to the changes. Grasslands can become deserts, and wetlands can become flooded.

As well as the air, the oceans are warming too. This can be fatal for some sea creatures. Coral reefs are very sensitive ecosystems that are especially endangered, becoming bleached and lifeless in high temperatures. Read more about the issues facing wildlife on the next page.

Losing living things

What do you think of flies? And how do you feel about wasps? Many people don't like creepy crawlies, but wasps and flies are just a couple of many different types of living thing that are very important to us, but are under threat.

Dying off

The current rate of extinction – meaning how often a species goes extinct – is 1,000 times higher than it naturally should be. Scientists estimate that 150–200 species of plant, insect, bird and mammal become extinct every 24 hours. One of the biggest threats to wildlife is destruction of the habitats where they live.

Land use

Human beings take up a lot of space. We are currently using over a third of the world's land to produce food for ourselves. But cutting down forests and clearing natural landscapes to make space for farming or buildings destroys the habitats of other living things.

The friends we need

Killing off so many plant and animal species isn't just bad news for them. It's bad news for us, too. Remember — we are part of Earth's natural systems. Flies, wasps and other flying insects pollinate our food. We need them to be able to grow things like chocolate, apples and tea.

Pollinate

Insects, birds, bats and the wind take pollen between flowering plants. This helps the plant reproduce and grow fruit.

Disappearing fish

Likewise, human beings rely on healthy oceans: three billion people in the world depend on both wild-caught and farmed seafood as their main source of protein. But currently, we are taking fish out of the ocean faster than they can reproduce, threatening their populations. Read about another threat to the oceans on pages 14–15.

Be a bee

Understand how our pollinators are under threat with this game.

How to play

Find a die, and five counters to represent your five wild bees. One counter at a time, try to make your way across the board, rolling the die to see how many spaces to move forward. Any time one of your counters lands on a LOSE square, take it off the board, and start again with a new counter.

Will any of your five bees make it to the end of summer?

Start here

1

2. You are a ground-nesting bee, but your nesting area has been paved over. LOSE.

3

4

5. You have found a tiny patch of suitable habitat to nest. But it is surrounded by ploughed fields, where all the wildflowers containing the nectar you eat have been removed. You can't find any food. LOSE.

6

7

Congratulations! You've survived!

23

22

21. You catch a bee disease that humans accidentally spread into the country. LOSE.

20

17. No other bees of your species have survived locally, so you can't find a mate. LOSE.

19

18

16

15

14

13. It's late summer. The farmer's crops are flowering, so there is lots of food around. But the crops have been covered in insect-killing pesticides! LOSE.

12

11

9. You're trying to stock your nest with pollen for your young. But climate change means flowers aren't blooming and producing pollen at the correct time. LOSE.

10

8

Problems with pollution

Pollution is the release of harmful gases, liquids and solid materials into the environment. Pollution has a range of damaging effects on our health, and the health of the natural world.

Air pollution

Factories and the engines in our vehicles release smoke and other toxic gases such as nitrogen oxides into the air. As well as carbon dioxide which causes the greenhouse effect, other types of air pollution can cause health problems such as breathing difficulties, and can harm the health of plants and animals.

Water pollution

Chemicals and litter can be washed or released into waterways such as rivers and the ocean, poisoning aquatic wildlife. Chemicals from factories and farming, and oil spills are all leading causes of water pollution – but one of the most widespread problems is plastic pollution.

Ocean plastic

Plastic is light, versatile, strong and cheap to make. As a result, we produce about 300 million tonnes of plastic around the world each year. But only 10 per cent of it is recycled, and up to 12 million tonnes find their way into the sea every year – that's a rubbish truck load every minute. If nothing changes, by 2050 there will be more plastic (by weight) in the ocean than fish.

Recycling
The process of treating waste materials so they can be reused.

Deadly to animals

Plastic doesn't break down, and fish and birds eat tiny bits of plastic by mistake. Birds end up with stomachs full of plastic, and turtles choke on plastic bags.

To solve the problem of plastic pollution in the ocean, we must all try to avoid using disposable plastics, and be careful to recycle the plastic we do use.

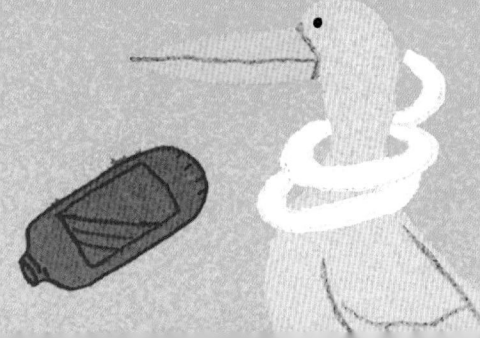

One planet living

How big is your footprint? Not the one from your actual foot! Your 'ecological footprint' is a way to understand the amount of environmental resources (such as land and water) that are needed to produce the food you eat, the stuff you own and the energy you use.

Very big feet

At the moment, the Earth's population is using up the planet's resources in an unsustainable way. But some people use many more resources than others. For example, if everyone in the world lived the same lifestyle as the average Australian, we would need around five planet Earths to support us. On the other hand, if everyone lived like the average Vietnamese person, we could live sustainably on a planet that was around 10 per cent smaller.

Sustainable living
Living in a way that we can continue to do forever, without using up the Earth's resources or harming the environment.

Footprint calculator

There are lots of websites where you can calculate how big your own ecological footprint is, and how many planet Earths are needed to maintain your lifestyle. Search online for 'ecological footprint calculator' to find one.

Eco diary

Calculating your ecological footprint should also give you some ideas of how you could start reducing your impact on the environment. Keep a diary of any environmentally friendly activities that you do. Entries could include:

★ Choosing eco-friendly transport such as walking, cycling or public transport instead of getting a lift in the car.

★ Eating less meat and dairy, as most plant-based foods require less land and water to produce.

★ Reusing and recycling objects and waste.

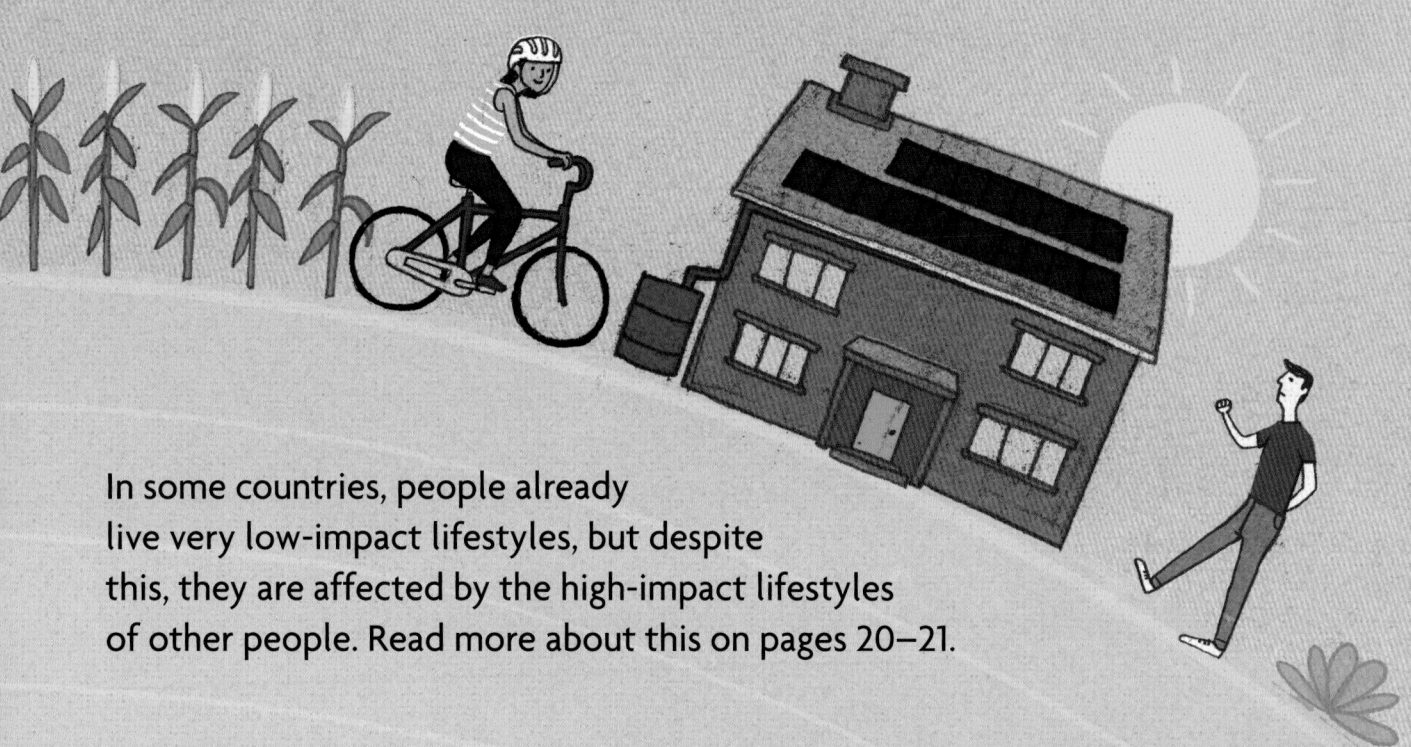

In some countries, people already live very low-impact lifestyles, but despite this, they are affected by the high-impact lifestyles of other people. Read more about this on pages 20–21.

Big green quiz

The problems facing the environment are serious, but we can do something about them. How much do you know about what we can do differently?

1. Most CO_2 is released when we burn fossil fuels to generate energy such as electricity. Which of these two things would result in a bigger saving of CO_2?
a) Turning your laptop off when you aren't using it
b) Buying a second-hand laptop instead of a new one

2. Not taking flights is one way to save a lot of CO_2. But do you know what the most impactful change most people can make to reduce the amount of carbon dioxide they are responsible for?
a) Eating plant-based foods instead of meat or dairy
b) Turning down the heating or air-conditioning at home

3. Recycling materials saves a lot of energy compared to making things from scratch. How much energy is saved by recycling metal items rather than making new ones?
a) 95 per cent
b) 65 per cent

4. Switching to public transport, walking and cycling instead of going by car saves a lot of CO_2. Can you guess how much it saves on average per year?
a) 1 tonne, the same as having the TV on for 250 days solid
b) 2.4 tonnes, the same as powering a light bulb continuously for 21 years

5. Farmland covers a lot of the planet, and the way that land is managed makes the difference between helping and hurting wildlife. What sort of food is best to buy?
a) Organic, locally-grown produce
b) Tinned and preserved food that lasts longer

6. Every small change that you can make to help the environment is important. But do you know what thing people can do that makes the biggest difference of all?
a) Having fewer children
b) Not travelling by aeroplane

Feeling stumped? The answers to these questions are on page 32.

What is environmental justice?

What do you think the phrase 'environmental justice' means? You probably know that justice means 'fairness', or getting what you deserve. So how can we think about 'fairness' when it comes to the environment?

Environmental needs

We all depend on the environment to provide us with a safe and healthy place to live, as well as resources such as food and water. Environmental justice is the idea that everyone should share these resources fairly — and that the impact of any environmental problems should be shared equally too.

Yet around the world, it's often the people who are least to blame for climate change or pollution who suffer the biggest impact.

Climate injustice

Most of the CO_2 that has been released into the atmosphere over the last 250 years is from a small number of rich countries and regions. Together, the five biggest emitters — the United States, the European Union, China, Russia and Japan — account for over two-thirds of all CO_2 emissions in history.

However, due to the differences in global weather patterns, it is the poorest countries such as low-lying Bangladesh and many African countries, who have not contributed much to the greenhouse gas emissions, that are already being hardest hit by flooding, drought and food shortages.

Billions of people around the world can't afford to own cars, eat a lot of meat and dairy, take flights abroad or buy lots of things. This is why their ecological footprints are smaller. It is essential that we reduce the amount of greenhouse gases going into the atmosphere to combat climate change — but does that mean poor people should never be allowed the lifestyles that people in richer countries enjoy?

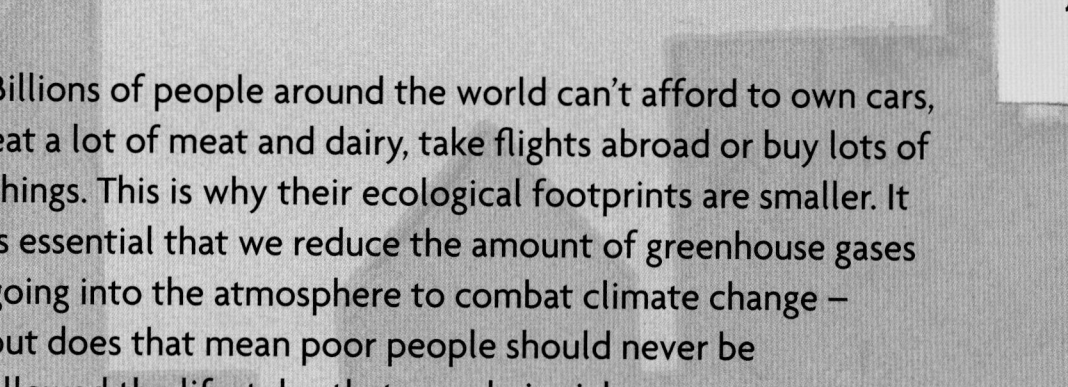

Making change happen: The Paris Agreement

Climate change is a big problem, so why haven't countries done more to prevent it? At the moment, about 80 per cent of the world's energy comes from fossil fuels which release greenhouse gases, and cause climate change.

Climate change and money

Around the world, many people make their money by making, selling and buying new goods such as clothes, toys and electronics, made in factories which release greenhouse gases. This means that for many countries, it is a challenge to reduce their emissions and still keep their economy going, which provides people with jobs and wages.

Economy
The system of how money is made and used in a particular country or region.

Countries coming together

No single country can fix the problem alone. Everyone around the world must work together. In 1995, the first United Nations Climate Change Conference was held. These conferences happen each year, and countries discuss what action can be taken to combat climate change. The discussions are often difficult, with countries disagreeing about how much responsibility they each need to take to reduce their own emissions.

The Paris Agreement

In 2016, the conference was held in Paris. After many years' work negotiating, 195 countries agreed on a deal to take action against climate change. A key part of the agreement is that each country has their own specific targets, because a one-size-fits-all approach wouldn't be fair when wealthy countries who have been polluting the longest can start using renewable energy without harming their economies. According to the agreement, wealthy countries will also help poorer countries switch to renewable energy.

There is still a lot more work to be done to combat climate change, but the Paris Agreement is an important first step.

Profile: Wangari Maathai

Wangari Maathai was born on 1 April 1940, in a little village in the Kenyan countryside. She was very clever, and although it wasn't usual for poor, rural girls in Kenya at that time, her parents sent her to school. She did very well, and in 1960 she won a scholarship to study biology at university in the USA. She later returned to Kenya, and became the first female lecturer at the University of Nairobi.

Through volunteering with organisations such as the Kenya Red Cross Society and the United Nations Environment Programme, Wangari saw that many people in Kenya were suffering due to a lack of firewood and water. Without firewood, people could not cook healthy food, which caused malnutrition.

She realised that these problems arose because so many trees had been cut down to make space for crops, such as tea, that could be sold for money. But without the trees to keep the soil stable, water quickly ran off the land. This caused a lack of water, eroded the soil – making it hard to grow food, and also meant there was no wood for cooking with.

The solution? Plant trees. In 1977, she started a movement that helped local women to plant native trees. This was called the Green Belt Movement. It became very successful. Since it started, over 51 million trees have been planted in Kenya, and over 30,000 women have been trained in forestry skills.

Alongside her environmental work, Wangari also helped women register to vote and pushed to improve Kenya's political system. At the time, the government was very undemocratic, and tried to stop her. However, they did not succeed. The Green Belt Movement grew and grew, and in 2004 Wangari was awarded the Nobel Peace Prize for her contribution to sustainable development, democracy and peace.

Activate!
Be a photojournalist

Journalists tell people about important news and current issues. Telling a news story visually through photographs with captions is called photojournalism.

By showing pictures of an issue or news story, it can help bring it to life. Actually seeing a problem is often more powerful than reading about it. For example, seeing a picture of an elephant struggling to find water can have more impact than reading statistics about the impact of drought on elephant populations.

Challenge

Find an environmental issue or news story that is relevant to where you live. It could centre on a problem, such as how lots of litter ends up on the local beach. Or, you could focus on a positive news story about people taking steps to improve the environment – perhaps there is a project helping wildlife in your area?

Research your story online and by talking to people. Think about what pictures you could take to show people the story visually. For example, for a story on rubbish in the ocean you could take a photograph of some litter that has washed ashore.

When you have a series of photos that express your story, write some captions to go with them. These should say what is in the photos, and explain to your audience the most important points the photos are showing. You could upload your photos and captions to social media, or print them out and display them gallery-style along a wall.

Organise! Eco challenges

Inspire your friends and family to be friendly to the environment by appealing to their competitive spirit. Try these challenges and award prizes to whoever does the best.

There are so many environmental benefits to growing all kinds of plants. A growing challenge is a brilliant way to help nature. Try one of the following:

Food

Homegrown food doesn't have to be transported or packaged, and it can be grown in a way that doesn't harm insects and other wildlife. Who can grow the most food in a set amount of space (such as a 1-metre square)?

Flowers

Planting flowers is a fantastic way to help wildlife, because many insects feed on nectar and pollen. Challenge your friends to grow the prettiest and most flower-rich window box display.

zero waste challenge

Going totally waste-free is tough, but worth trying! See if you can avoid eating any snacks that come in disposable packaging and using plastic straws, plastic bags and anything else that creates waste for a week. If you do use something with disposable packaging, hang on to the packet. At the end of the week, everyone weighs their waste – the person with the least wins!

Car-free challenge

A lot of the time we travel by car when we could make the journey by foot, bike or public transport instead. Challenge your friends to go car-free for a month, if they have safe alternatives. Get everyone to tot up how many kilometres they travel without a car, and with a car. Whoever has the highest percentage of car-free travel is the winner.

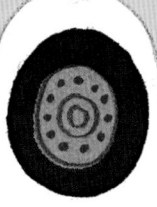

Glossary

atmosphere the layer of gases that surround our planet

climate change changes in world weather patterns caused by human activity

democracy a type of government where everyone votes for who they want in power

ecological footprint the amount of resources such as land, water and clean air that each person uses to live their lifestyle

economy the system of how money is made and used in a particular region or country

ecosystem all of the living things, such as plants, and non-living things, such as rocks, that are in a particular area, and the ways they interact with each other

emissions something that is being given off, particularly greenhouse gases

environment the physical surroundings on Earth, including plants, rocks, air, animals, rivers and so on

environmental justice the idea that everyone should equally share the benefits of a healthy environment, or the problems of an unhealthy environment

fossil fuels a fuel such as oil or coal that was formed over millions of years from the remains of plants and animals

greenhouse gases gases that, when in the atmosphere, trap more of the Sun's heat

habitat where a particular plant or animal lives

malnutrition poor health caused by not enough food, or not enough healthy food

pollinate when a living thing or the wind carry pollen from one plant to another, helping the plants to reproduce

pollution waste or chemicals that get into the environment and are harmful to people, plants or animals

recycling taking things or materials that have already been used, and making them into new things

renewable energy energy from a source that will never run out, such as the Sun or wind

scholarship money awarded to pay for someone's education

sustainable something that can be done in the same way forever without harming the environment

undemocratic where the people of a country have little or no control over the government

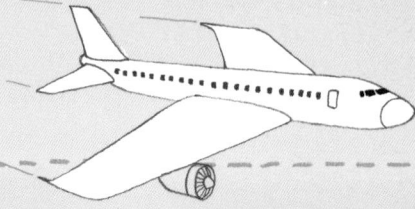

Further information

Go Green!
by Liz Gogerly (Franklin Watts, 2018)
Discover a range of hands-on ways that you can take action to help save the environment and the planet, from recycling to walking to school.

Question it! Climate Change
by Philip Steele (Wayland, 2017)
This book looks at climate change, what it is, what its impacts are and what causes it.

Eco STEAM series
by Georgia Amson-Bradshaw (Wayland, 2018)
A series of books about about sustainability and climate change issues. The books look at our diets, housing, cities, shopping habits and more, and how they imapct the environment, as well as how we could do things differently to be more eco-friendly.

Websites

www.exploratorium.edu/climate
This mini-site from the Exploratorium museum explains various systems on our planet such as the water cycle and the biosphere, and how these are affected by climate change.

www.plasticpollutioncoalition.org
The website of a global movement against plastic pollution in our oceans. Read about the facts, and find out how you can take action.

www.rootsandshoots.org
An organisation set up by Jane Goodall, helping children and young people to start their own campaigns to help wildlife, the environment and people. Find information on the website on how to set up your own campaign, or join other campaigns run by young people.

Note to parents and teachers: every effort has been made by the Publishers to ensure websites are suitable for children, that they are of the highest educational value, and that they contain no inappropriate or offensive material. However, because of the nature of the Internet, it is impossible to guarantee that the contents of these sites will not be altered. We strongly advise that Internet access is supervised by a responsible adult.

Index

Answers to pages 18–19: 1, b – the energy a laptop uses to run is a lot less than the amount of energy it takes to make it in the first place. **2, a** – meat and dairy-heavy diets produce a lot of CO_2. Animals need a lot of land and eat a lot of food, which drives deforestation (cutting down trees). Cutting down trees and ploughing soil to grow animal feed releases CO_2 into the air. Also, the burps from cows and sheep are a powerful greenhouse gas! Going vegetarian can cut the average person's carbon footprint in half. Turning down the heating (or the air conditioning) is still useful though. **3, a. 4, b. 5** – this is a bit of a trick question! Organic, locally grown food is good because it doesn't use wildlife-harming pesticides and doesn't require as much energy to transport. However, food waste is bad for the environment too, so if using tinned foods helps someone waste less, that's a good thing. **6, a** – most people know that flying isn't very eco-friendly. Planes burn a lot of fuel, and the emissions in their exhausts are extra harmful because they are released straight into the layer of the atmosphere where it causes the greenhouse effect. However, having fewer children has the biggest impact of all, because each child produces so much CO_2 throughout the course of their life.